PHYLLIS NAGY

Phyllis Nagy was born in New York City and now lives in London. Her work includes *Trip's Cinch*, commissioned and produced by the Actors Theatre of Louisville, March 1994; an adaptation of Nathaniel Hawthorne's *The Scarlet Letter*, commissioned and produced by the Denver Center Theatre Company, March 1994; *Weldon Rising* (Royal Court Theatre, London, Liverpool Playhouse, Lubeck Theatre, Germany); and the Mobil prizewinning *Disappeared* (Midnight Theatre Company, UK, to be produced later in 1994).

Phyllis Nagy is currently writing *The Strip* for the Royal Court Theatre and a radio version for BBC Radio 4; *Never Land* for the Hampstead Theatre; and a feature-length film for the BBC, *The Night They Buried Judy Garland*. She recently completed a teleplay *Bait and Switch*, also for the BBC. Phyllis has received two playwriting fellowships from the National Endowment for the Arts, and has been awarded playwriting fellowships from the McKnight Foundation and the New York Foundation for the Arts. She is a member of New Dramatists.

A Selection of Other Volumes in this Series

*Published by Theatre Communications Group, distributed by Nick Hern Books

PHYLLIS NAGY

BUTTERFLY KISS

NICK HERN BOOKS
London

A Nick Hern Book

Butterfly Kiss first published in Great Britain
as a paperback original by Nick Hern Books,
14 Larden Road, London W3 7ST

Butterfly Kiss copyright © 1994 by Phyllis Nagy

Typeset by Country Setting, Woodchurch, Kent TN26 3TB
Printed by Cox and Wyman Ltd, Reading, Berks

Front cover illustration by Halpin Grey Vermeir

Lines from *My Melancholy Baby*, music by Ernie Burnett and words
by George Norton, Maybelle E. Watson, copyright © 1912 Shapiro
Bernstein and Co Inc, USA, and *Shine on Harvest Moon*, music by
Nora Bayes and words by Jack Norworth, copyright © 1908
Remick Music Corp, USA; reproduced by courtesy of Francis Day
and Hunter Ltd, London WC2H 0EA

A CIP catalogue record for this book is available from
the British Library

ISBN 1 85459 251 3

The Setting is a jail cell. Lily's memories of events transform the cell into many places: a lower-Manhattan kitchen; Jones Beach in November; a women's bar; a waterfront house in Queens; a Manhattan hi-rise; a patio in Fort Lauderdale, Florida. It is not necessary to present the cell as strictly realistic; however, the *sense* of present place must be recognisable as a jail cell.

The Time is the present, the past, the imagined past and the imagined future. Although Lily's age ranges substantially during the course of the play, no attempt should be made to 'play' the younger ages.

Characters

LILY ROSS.   A small, dark woman in her mid-to-late 20s with a splendidly dry and ironic sense of humour.

JENNY ROSS.   Lily's mother, mid-to-late 40s. A mild hypochondriac, lusty, rather beautiful and neurotically thin. She has a stunning singing voice.

SALLY RAMONA.   Lily's grandmother, mid-to-late 60s. Meaner than she thinks she is, chiefly because she completely lacks sentimentality. Doesn't realise how funny she is.

SLOAN ROSS.   Lily's father, mid-to-late 40s. An intriguing personality contradiction: sexy and handsome in a remote yet gentle way; academic yet un-professorial; cold yet sympathetic; imposing yet ineffectual. He will never let his working class roots betray him.

MARTHA McKENZIE.   Lily's lover, 35ish. Crisp, nononsense approach to all thing cannot hide a flirtatious and quite light aspect to her dealings with Lily. Sexy and rather feminine, with a highly developed sense of irony.

CHRISTINE, THE COUNTESS VAN DYNE.   Sloan's lover, late 40s. A born-and-bred New Yorker from Howard Beach, Queens, who, while very young married a dubious European count and then deserted him. Faux elegant and naive in the most unassuming way. Speaks with a pronounced Queens accent.

TEDDY ROOSEVELT HAYES.   Lily's first lover, mid-to-late 40s. An ex-U.S. Marine who's big, handsome, and somewhat slow on the uptake. Sweeter and more polite than one would expect.

JACKSON TROUVER.   Lily's attorney, 35ish. A thoroughly charming and cynical raconteur.

Butterfly Kiss was first performed at the Almeida Theatre, London, on 7 April 1994, with the following cast:

LILY ROSS	Elizabeth Berridge
JENNY ROSS	Susan Brown
SALLY RAMONA	Mary Macleod
SLOAN ROSS	Oliver Cotton
MARTHA MCKENZIE	Debora Weston
CHRISTINE, THE COUNTESS VAN DYNE	Sandra Dickinson
TEDDY ROOSEVELT HAYES	Larry Lamb
JACKSON TROUVER	Andrew Woodall

Directed by Steven Pimlott
Designed by Mark Thompson
Lighting by Hugh Vanstone

Act One

LILY (*to the audience*). Of course, what's always been the
most interesting to me is the Halls-Mills trial of 1926.
Testifying from a portable hospital bed, Jane Gibson, also
known as the pig woman, accused Mrs. Halls and her
brothers of murder.

Lights up on SALLY *and* JENNY. JENNY *wears a slinky*
black cocktail dress. She sips at some scotch. Wrapped
tightly around her right arm is the sleeve of a blood
pressure pump. SALLY, *while watching television,*
nonchalantly squeezes the little black air pump.

SALLY. Look at this, Jenny. They got Jackie O's doctor on.

JENNY. Imagine that.

LILY. The defence counsel, however, proved Miss Gibson to
be a most unreliable witness. She could not remember who
or when and where she had married, or whether or not she
had, indeed, been divorced.

SALLY. You was a pain in the ass when we took that drive out
to the Boo-vee-ay mansion. Phil and crazy Figgy driving us
in a storm. Out to some house we wasn't sure we could find.
You was a real fucking pain.

JENNY. My arm. Not so tight, mother.

SALLY. Pregnant and screaming with the bulk of it, you were.
I said – and I remember perfectly well saying this to you – I
said: HEY. YOU STUPID ENOUGH TO KNOCK YOUR-
SELF UP WITH TROUBLE, YOU BETTER BE SMART
ENOUGH TO BITE THE BULLET OF MOTHERHOOD
WITHOUT COMPLAINING. Yeah. Ruined my chance to
catch a glimpse of some old rich lady at a window. Long
yellow fingernail scratching against a pane of glass.

JENNY. You're hurting my arm.

SALLY. Yeah? Maybe I'll pop a vessel. Would you like that, Jenny?

LILY. The Halls-Mills case remained unsolved. Mrs. Halls and her brothers were acquitted, courtesy of the pig woman. My name is Lily Ross. I may be less fortunate.

JENNY. My pressure's 140 over 90. You're probably making it go up 50, 60 points.

SALLY. Bullshit. I'm pumping some life into your arm. Hey: wouldn't it be something if Lily married John-John Kennedy? They're Catholic, ain't they? What will you wear to the wedding?

JENNY. Black.

SALLY. He's a *smart* guy. He's gonna get himself a university education. And money. Lily'd buy us a house in Florida. Big brick house with a portable patio.

LILY. Or consider the case of Bela Kiss, a Hungarian tinsmith who murdered his wife and her lover in 1912. Over the following fifteen years, Mr. Kiss advertised for new wives. He killed twenty-one women, mostly by strangulation, and took the bodies to his cellar, where he kept them in drums. The bodies floated in alcohol.

JENNY. I like New York. Sloan likes New York.

SALLY. I'm *tired* of New York. What I need is SUNSHINE. If your husband don't like Florida, leave him here. Lily's gonna take care of us.

JENNY. Lily's not interested in buying houses. And how do you know John-John Kennedy will like the idea of Florida? Look: my pressure's up. I'm getting sick. Give me some more scotch.

LILY. Mr. Kiss' crimes were discovered at the outbreak of World War I, which proved to be a most welcome diversion for him. Bela Kiss vanished during the war.

SALLY. Well. Then forget about Lily. Who needs her? She'll buy the house with the blue-blood's money. We'll live there.

JENNY. Have a drink with me, okay?

SALLY. Not me. But you go ahead. Keeps you quiet.

JENNY. You could drink me under any table.

LILY. I work in a small gift shop at the South Street Seaport. The kind of place that attracts Canadian tourists. I'm interested in composition. Musical composition, that is.

SALLY. I could leave you here, you know that. Let you rot in place. Shrivel up with a shot glass in one hand and a blood pressure kit in the other. I shrivel little by little myself, just thinking about how I could have given birth to something like you.

JENNY. I'm not so bad.

SALLY. You're a vegetable in a party dress.

JENNY. Where's Lily?

SALLY. She's probably reading something. Kid's got no sense.

LILY (*holding out her arms to* JENNY). Mama.

JENNY. Lily-pie, come over here and brush your mama's hair.

SALLY (*still watching tv*). Goddamn. It's that good-looking Tony Tucci. He's real *old* now. Went berserk after his younger sister shot up the older sister. You remember Tony Tucci?

LILY (*approaching* JENNY). Give me the brush, mama.

JENNY. Hiya, Lily. Your grandma won't drink with me. But maybe you'd like to.

SALLY. Phil and me went to her trial. She never would say why she did it. It was really *something*. Tina wore such nice clothes at her trial. Made a strong impression on the jury. I could tell. But not strong enough, 'cause they sent her to the chair, anyway. If only she woulda said why she did it. *I* understood. Her sister wasn't no joy to look at every day. Yeah. Nice looking fella, that Tony Tucci.

LILY. I'm not old enough to drink, mama.

JENNY. Nonsense, Lily-pie. The females in our line got the

booze gene. Your own grandma started hitting the bottle at age two. Pint after pint of Gordon's in her baby bottle. Why, from the moment I escaped from her womb, she breast fed me gin.

SALLY. So what if I did? Maybe I gave you the only thrill of your life. So what.

LILY. I don't believe you, grandma. It's impossible to breast feed a child on liquor.

SALLY. Fancy talk. You read that in some book?

JENNY. You read all you like, Lily. If you're not born pretty you might as well read. Or drink.

LILY. I'm too young to drink.

JENNY. Don't you think I look like Tallulah Bankhead when I wear this dress?

JACKSON TROUVER *enters. He addresses the audience.*

JACKSON. Consider the case of my client, ladies and gentlemen. Lily Ramona Ross. Aged . . . twenty-something and three months. Born under the sign of the scorpion. For those of you who are interested . . . in that sort of thing.

JENNY. Really, Lily. People tell me I look like her all the time. When I wear black, especially.

LILY. I'm too young to remember Tallulah Bankhead.

JACKSON. Don't you think it's curious how people are always interested in analysing a murderer's motive by way of, oh, astrological data and such?

SALLY. Tallulah Bankhead my ASS. Sam Jaffe's more like it. Oh, Lily, Sam Jaffe was out of this WORLD. A very fine actor.

LILY. I've never heard of him.

SALLY. Yeah. Well, he played mostly loonies. Played your mother once.

JACKSON. Got a call one morning from my college buddy, Martha McKenzie.

MARTHA *enters*.

MARTHA (*she, too, addresses the audience*). My lover is in trouble, Jackson.

JACKSON. She says to me, Jackson, my lover is in trouble.

JENNY. Your father likes me in black. Don't you like me in black, Lily?

LILY. You look . . . thinner.

JENNY. I'm fat? You think I'm fat? I'm not fat.

SALLY. Nah, Lily. She's not fat. Sam Jaffe was *thin*. Forget about her, Lily. Think about *me*. Why don't you go on one of those game shows and make us a bunch of money?

JACKSON. Martha's a photographer. Mostly travel assignments. We went to school together. And when she told me of Lily Ross' . . . circumstances . . . I could not refuse. It's what is called a once-in-a-lifetime case.

MARTHA. She's been arrested, Jackson. They say she's murdered her mother.

JACKSON. Jackson, she says, my lover's killed her mother.

JENNY. I've lost a lot of weight, Lily. I have. My pressure rises and my weight drops. It's the damnedest thing. And your father says I have to wear something . . . presentable . . . to his lectures. I think I look elegant in black. To hell with the rest of you.

SALLY. Isn't it about time you took another pressure reading, Jenny? Who knows. Maybe you got real sick while you wasn't looking. What about it Lily? A game show to make a fast buck?

LILY (*to* JENNY). I like you better in bright colours. Pastels. Why don't you wear pink?

JENNY. What do *you* know, Lily? Your father likes me in black. Go on. Read up on Tallulah for me, baby.

MARTHA. It happens while I am in Africa. When I return to New York, I find a note from Sloan Ross. It says, simply: CALL ME. Lily's clothes were gone. Her bookcases filled

only with dust. Darker white patches on the bright white
walls where her paintings had hung. I didn't particularly
want to speak with Sloan Ross. He was always a difficult
man.

JACKSON. Let us say that Sloan Ross is not fond of my
photographer friend.

SALLY. It's always other people's kids who are raking in the
dough on t.v. But I got a hunch about you, Lily-doll. And if
you don't win a bundle on Hollywood Squares, I was
thinking you could marry one of the Kennedys.

JACKSON. Martha spends a quarter on a call to the noted
professor, Sloan Ross.

MARTHA. Hello, Mr. Ross. This is Martha McKenzie. Your
note requests that I call.

JACKSON. I pay a visit to the Ross residence. The place has
been mobbed for hours, this normally quiet walk-up where
people claim to keep to themselves and say their hellos at
the mailboxes. In theory, people think it's best to keep to
themselves. In practice, common sense prevails.

MARTHA. And he says, Miss McKenzie, it's very good of you
to call. Like he's talking to one of his students. Said he was
quite busy now, but that if I would call Lily at such-and-
such a number, she'd be happy to explain. Then he hung up.

LILY. I don't think I can marry a Kennedy, grandma. They live
in Boston.

JENNY. Lily. Lily-sweet. I'm feeling light-headed. My heart's
beating real fast. Where's my chart? Give me my chart, honey.

JACKSON. The Ross apartment is not large. Cops all over,
blue abounding. Takes me a while to get through the crowd.
When finally I'm inside, I'm overwhelmed by the presence
of white things. White appliances, wallpaper, linoleum.
Very clean. Almost antiseptic.

MARTHA. I call such-and-such a number to reach Lily. The
line's busy. Once, a man answers and mumbles something
about a precinct. I hang up. How am I supposed to know that
Lily's been arrested?

JACKSON. And there's this cluster of blue uniforms in the kitchen. This white kitchen. Upon closer inspection, one notices splotches of red on all that white. Blood. There's blood seeping out of every corner. But it's splattered in bits. So that it seems hidden. Or lost.

SALLY. Here we go again, Lily. Your mama thinks you been paying your grandma too much attention. Go on. Take care of her.

SALLY gives LILY a small chalkboard. A piece of chalk is attached to the board with a string. On the board are neatly written rows of figures: JENNY's charting of her own blood pressure.

LILY. Mama . . . I don't . . . I'm afraid to do this.

JENNY. I need you now.

SALLY. That's right, Lily. Your mama don't feel right if that thing ain't pumped against her arm every twenty minutes. You're a big girl, Lily. It's time you learned your function here.

MARTHA. I try again. The same officer answers and I know I haven't dialled wrong. It's a long time before I actually speak with Lily. I was transferred quite a bit, you see, and I could taste the distance between us through the telephone lines. As if each transfer, each click of each switchboard, took me deeper underground. Under something I could not accept.

JACKSON. I don't stay at the Ross apartment. It's too much, you know, with Sally Ramona on her hands and knees, scrubbing at non-existent blood stains. A homicide detective told me she'd been at it for three days. Ever since the body'd been removed. There was a woman wearing a blue night-gown in the hallway outside of the apartment.

LILY. I might hurt her.

SALLY. You won't. Don't you think I've tried? Listen to me. She ain't got pain cells.

LILY takes her mother's blood pressure.

JENNY. That's it. More. I feel it making me right.

LILY *pumps too hard.* JENNY *slaps her.*

JACKSON. This lady in blue's slugging down a bottle of Gordon's. She's doing a jig and singing that song about Lizzie Borden and her axe.

MARTHA. When I get through to Lily, she is not hysterical.

JENNY (*to* LILY). Don't come near me.

SALLY *takes the blood pressure pump from* LILY.

SALLY. Why don't you go read something, Lily? Guess I was wrong about not being able to hurt her. You learn something new about your kids every day.

JACKSON. I don't know why, but watching that woman do her grisly number in the hallway strikes me as the funniest thing I've seen in years. Red, white and blue this place is. Like a flag. And a drunken woman singing songs about a suspected hatchet murderess. It's all very . . . American.

MARTHA. Her voice does not crack. She says –

LILY. Please, mama. Please listen to me.

MARTHA. – mama, please. That's all. She hangs up. Very quietly. As if she is putting down a teacup. It occurs to me that it's the second time this day a member of the Ross family has cut me off.

JENNY. Leave us be, sweetheart. Your grandma knows how to bring me up. Leave us alone.

SALLY *cradles* JENNY's *head in one arm, strokes her hair. She takes* JENNY's *blood pressure with her free hand.*

Lights down on SALLY *and* JENNY.

JACKSON. But that woman forgot one thing. Lizzie Borden was acquitted. Like I said, the Ross case seems to be a big one. So I take it. Martha's got substantial amounts of cash.

JACKSON *exits.*

MARTHA. Do you have what you need, Lily? Is it . . . I don't know . . . comfortable enough?

LILY. I've been reading a lot lately. Sensational crime cases. Mostly murder cases. There's a vested interest, I'll admit.

MARTHA. Would you like to talk with a doctor? Anybody?

LILY. I thought I'd write an opera.

MARTHA. It wouldn't be difficult to get somebody in here. Jackson could help.

LILY. Last week I thought it might be a string quartet. A lovely piece of action for violins. But now I think it must be a vocal piece. In a minor key.

MARTHA. You're serious.

LILY. I am. Are you familiar with the Harvard microbiologist who killed her parents? She was very young, and very smart. She had a future.

MARTHA. No, Lily. I don't know about her. Would you please talk to somebody? It doesn't have to be me. I just want to know that you're fine.

LILY. Putting on some weight, aren't you?

MARTHA. I stay home and read newspaper articles about you. I eat fudge. I miss you. I *like* fudge.

LILY. So. This very smart microbiologist, armed with graduate degrees from the nation's most prestigious university, can't find a job. Can you believe it?

MARTHA. I can't tell you how painful it is to read those stories. Strangers speculating about your past. Men who sit behind computer terminals for a living, playing their hunches about what makes you tick.

LILY. Miss microbiologist returns home. Unemployed, fat and most unhappy. She eats peppermint twists while her mother works at an A & P. One day, she uses her impressive education to assemble her father's shotgun. She'd never before touched a gun.

MARTHA. Nobody has an answer, Lily. They say you're not insane. But no one wants to believe that. I'm not sure *what* I believe.

LILY. And then she waits for her mother to come home. Mom walks in and her hulk of a spawn blows her away. Turns out mommy's little girl is a crack shot. She gets her father soon after. He's napping and doesn't have a chance to contemplate what a monster he's created.

MARTHA. Lily, I've been thinking I should go away. I've been offered an assignment in Germany.

LILY. Our heroine is judged to be criminally insane and is packed off to a state institution. Ten uneventful years pass. Miss Harvard becomes the subject of a television interview. Mr. Newsman asks her if she is prepared, ten years after the fact, to talk about her motives. Dear, he says, a soothing modulated baritone, can you tell us why you did it?

MARTHA. I could wait for you, Lily. We would go together. Heidelberg. Munich. The Rhine.

LILY. Well. She looks right past our baritoned reporter, smiles, like she's a dowager empress amused by the efforts of her lady-in-waiting. There is no faraway look to her eyes. No glazing over. Foam is not in evidence at the corners of her mouth. She says, 'why, of course I can tell you what happened. My mother had a habit of going out every evening at the same time. She told me she'd be back within an hour, but each time she left she wouldn't return until the next morning.' You see, Martha, this poor soul hadn't a clue as to where her mommy went. All she knew was that mommy went out with the moon and came in with the sun.

MARTHA. Please think about it, Lily. I'm not sure I can be here much longer.

LILY. By this time, our t.v. interviewer is most uncomfortable. He doesn't have the upper hand. She's not crazy, after all. And even though she doesn't have a weapon, this huge man is afraid of her. There's a look in his eyes. She notices, of course, and concludes her explanation by saying that she allows her mother to do this for six successive evenings. On the seventh evening, she shoots her. She figures while she has the shotgun handy, she might as well take care of her pop. It was a perfectly plausible motive, Martha. And no one believed her. Mr. Newsman, faced with the woman's most remarkable candour, relaxes. He even slumps back in his chair. Sure, he thinks, she's out of her mind after all. Nothing to fear anymore.

MARTHA. I want you to write that opera, Lily. In a *major* key. I'll bring you music paper.

LILY. Bring me fudge.

MARTHA. I don't suppose . . . you'd talk to me about it.

LILY. You make the best fudge.

MARTHA. Well. I'm going home. I'll eat a lot. I'll read newspapers and refuse to answer my phone. I'll wait a while longer for you.

MARTHA *exits.*

Lights up on JENNY. *She wears her cocktail dress and armband, as before.*

JENNY. Lily, can you tell me what it is exactly a lepidopterist *does?* Honestly, when I met your daddy he was a soldier. He was just a regular guy. It was years later he took an interest in bugs. I was reading up on the subject of butterflies in an encyclopaedia yesterday. Really. I was. Sitting here in my old comfy chair while you were at school, reading, and listening to Billie Holiday, her sweet voice, and the telephone rings. Ring ring goes the telephone and you know, for a long time I think it's part of Billie's song. A ringing telephone is such an unfamiliar sound to me, honey. I can't get together the extra push, the rush of energy it takes to pull myself out of that chair. So I figure, why bother? It'll stop soon enough. But it doesn't stop. And so I throw all I've got into the act of getting up and I answer and the ringing stops and there's a voice. A female voice with an accent. The voice says to my telephone: *Bonjour.* May I *parler* with Sloan Ross? I say to myself, Jenny, who the hell is Sloan Ross? The female voice is . . . nervous. I can tell by the breathing. Very quick. In spurts. And then I remember. Well, *yeah*, Sloan Ross is the father of my baby. I try to answer the voice's question, but by that time it's gone. What's left for your mama to do but return to her chair? It's a funny thing, Lily. When I met your daddy, I was a

switchboard operator. The telephone was my line to
excitement. And I couldn't even keep a timid female voice
on the line. Well. It's better to sit in the dark and remember
nothing. If you sit in the dark long enough something
scary's bound to happen.

LILY. I'm right here, mama.

JENNY. Lily-pie, are you here? Did you say something about
dancing? That's nice.

LILY. No, mama. I was telling you . . . I was going to say that I
really do think you look nice in black.

JENNY. You shouldn't fib. But thanks all the same.

LILY. I found a picture of Tallulah Bankhead today. You do
look like her. In a way.

JENNY. Why don't you talk to me about dancing.

LILY. I've never been dancing.

JENNY. Don't be so *boring*, baby. That's what your daddy
says to me. Why don't you talk to me about *dancing*, he
says.

LILY. Mama, it's Lily. I'm here. Not him.

JENNY. It's not me anymore, Jennifer. I'm not the fella you
hitched up with. Why don't you wrap your arms around me
and DANCE?

JENNY *wraps her arms around* LILY. *She kisses* LILY's
neck. She begins to dance.

JENNY. Oh yeah. Yessss. Of course. So sweet, baby. So light
on your feet. Teach me what you know.

LILY *pushes* JENNY *away.*

LILY. I can't do this, mama. It's not right.

JENNY. What are you looking at? What? How come you're
looking at me that way?

LILY. I don't know. I . . . can't touch . . . you that way.

JENNY. Whatsa matter, Lily-pie. Too old to hold your mama.
Too smart.

LILY. I'm not him, mama.

JENNY. Who loves you best. Who loves you more.

LILY. I can't say.

JENNY. WHO LOVES YOU BEST.

LILY. You love me best.

JENNY. Who loves you more.

LILY. You. You, mama.

JENNY. And who's your sweetheart?

LILY. You're my sweetheart.

JENNY. And I'm the nicest person you know.

LILY. Yes.

JENNY. So. What have you got to tell me?

LILY (*hesitates, offers her hand to* JENNY). Would you . . . why don't you dance with me. Just a little.

JENNY. Yes, sugar. It's so nice of you to ask.

JENNY *and* LILY *dance in place. It's really more of an awkward and tentative hug, but they do try.*

JACKSON *enters. He addresses the audience.*

JACKSON. I've seen the evidence, the remainder, really, of most imaginable crimes. Many of my colleagues will tell you that a lawyer's success depends on how relatively unaffected he remains by the circumstances of his job. In truth, there's little that pulls at us or horrifies us because we are inevitably several steps removed from an actual crime. We do not look on while perps pull triggers. What we deal with is the aftermath of crime. And that's always . . . intellectually satisfying. Emotionally undemanding. And safe. Most of all it is safe, what we lawyers do. Of course, it is as it should be. We cannot risk emotional involvement with the crimes upon which our livelihood depends.

JENNY *exits.*

A perverse instinct, an instinct that verges on crime itself, propels our interest in lawbreakers. It's the desire to know what enables crime to exist, but not the naked crime, the knife in a back, that we court. Like a lust we're ashamed of but can't quite shake, we like to take crime into dark places with us. Not out into the sunlight. Everything looks better in the dark.

LILY *listens to* JACKSON.

JACKSON. I've lost only one case. A fifty-year-old baritone who had a Broadway credit a million years ago, gives singing lessons to co-eds in Arizona. He has a favourite student – don't they all, though – pretty blonde kid. Sweet sixteen. Kind of girl who's accused of having *promise*. He takes her to the top of a hill one sunny Arizona afternoon and tells her that altitude is good for the vocal chords. He presents her with a tape recorder, a big red bow scotch taped to its top. He gives her a tape of his Broadway show. She listens. She laughs. Perhaps she's nervous. Perhaps she's more sensitive to the sadness of this scene than he understands. So he strangles her. Cops find the recorder blasting Rodgers and Hammerstein at the scene of the crime.

I stood at the top of that hill, much later in the day, first cousin to crime, thrice removed. And the only remaining evidence of horror, the only trace of human involvement, was a chalk outline of that girl's body on grass. I lost the baritone's case. Do you have any idea of how difficult it is to lay down a chalk outline on grass?

LILY. Mama. Mama, where'd you go. I meant no harm.

JACKSON. Whatcha doing there, Lily?

LILY. I'm talking to the voices in my head.

JACKSON. All right. Perhaps you can convince those voices to have a chat with me.

LILY. Sorry, counsellor. They're shy. They don't like strangers.

JACKSON. Let's take it from the beginning.

LILY. I've been through the beginning. Let's get on to the end.

JACKSON. Start with Teddy Hayes.

LILY. What are my chances of springing this place?

JACKSON. None. Now. What about Teddy Hayes?

LILY. Listen. Martha's going to Europe. I'd like to go with her. So see what you can do for me.

JACKSON. I'd like to win this case.

LILY. I'd like you to win this case.

JACKSON. Good. Do you understand that if you keep your secrets to yourself, I don't win. You don't go bye-bye with Martha and nobody gets a picture postcard of Paris By Night.

LILY. Munich.

JACKSON. Uh-huh. Well. Tell me something about Teddy Hayes.

LILY. Teddy is the dumbest man I know. But I like him. He's sweet and uncomplicated.

TEDDY ROOSEVELT HAYES *enters.*

TEDDY (*to the audience*). Fourteen years old and smoother than a shot of scotch. Slim hips. Never looks you straight in the eye.

JACKSON. If he's so dumb, why did you fuck him?

LILY. Because, Jackson, like the mountain, he was there.

TEDDY. Jones Beach. Middle of November. Her daddy's fond of cold water. We have this reunion every year, same time and place, in celebration of our Marine days. Me and Sloan Ross go all the way back to Camp LeJeune. Before he went off to study butterflies. Bugs were a regular obsession with Sloanie.

JACKSON. Where and when did you meet Mr. Hayes?

LILY. I told you. I didn't exactly meet him. He was just . . . there.

JACKSON. Where? Be specific.

LILY. In the sand, of course.

TEDDY. So this one particular year Sloan brings his daughter

with him 'cause his wife is having one of her blood pressure
attacks or something. His goddamned *daughter*. I say, look
Sloan, it's real easy to offend a fourteen-year-old girl. Got
one of my own. And like I said, it's real easy to cross her.

JACKSON. Where was the sand, Lily? In a playground?

LILY. I don't know. Somewhere. It doesn't matter. He rose
from the sand like a monster. Muscled and wet and
shivering. He reminded me of something from a Japanese
horror film. I used to call him Mothra.

JACKSON. Did you seduce him?

LILY. Who can say, really? Sometimes I think my father
seduced Teddy for me.

JACKSON. Why would he do that?

LILY. My father is a scientist. He likes to watch.

Lights down on JACKSON.

TEDDY. I'm doing pushups on Jones Beach and believe me,
I'm trying to forget the cold. Up walks Sloan Ross and his
baby. I say to the baby, how do you do? I'm Teddy
Roosevelt Hayes and I'm an ex-Marine. She says, hi there,
Teddy, I'm Lily Ross. Do you think I'm fat? I'm staring at
this little girl with slim hips . . . but *real* slim . . . and all I
can picture is how she's gonna have one hell of a time in
childbirth with hips like those. I say to her, well, Lily, seems
to me you've got the slimmest hips this side of heaven and
she grins, leans in real close so I can see her tits and says,
well, Teddy, what do you think about THAT? Sloanie's
having a grand time embarrassing me in front of his kid. I
spend the whole day covering myself up with a beach towel.
Sloanie keeps asking, hey, Teddy, what's the deal with the
towel? Like he knows I'm hiding something. And I *am*.
Middle of November and this girl child with slim hips is
running around Jones Beach in a bathing suit. She's
collecting sea shells and wriggling her tight little ass in my
face. What was I supposed to do? I'm a pretty normal guy.
Never been arrested. Never taken much more than a social
drink. And I'd certainly never been moved to excitement by
fourteen-year-old buns. But Lily Ross . . . well. She was . . .

exciting to me. I tried to put it out of my mind. Sloanie knew what was going on. He probably planned it. Slim hips. My my my . . . Lily Ross was a sweetheart. Can't believe she went and popped her mommy off that way.

LILY. Teddy. Teddy Roosevelt Hayes. Are you really named after the Rough Rider?

TEDDY. Could be.

LILY. How come you don't know for sure?

TEDDY. Don't know. The subject never came up.

LILY. It's strange, Teddy. I mean, not knowing about your name. You're an ex-Marine.

TEDDY. That's right.

LILY. My father's an ex-Marine. Now he collects butterflies. Don't you think that's an interesting change of direction?

TEDDY. Your daddy's an interesting man.

LILY. Are you an interesting man, Teddy? I'm making small talk.

TEDDY. Uh-huh. Your daddy'll be back soon. And you won't have to fret about small talk.

LILY. No he won't. He's hunting specimens on the beach. When was the last time you found a butterfly on the beach?

TEDDY. I've never looked for one.

LILY. You have a daughter.

TEDDY. Yes.

LILY. What's her name?

TEDDY. Eleanor.

LILY. Nice name. Don't hear it much. Some names are more common than others. Take mine, for example. Very common. There's one in every kindergarten. Is your daughter pretty?

TEDDY. She's . . . pretty.

LILY. Is she prettier than me?

TEDDY. That's hard to say, Lily.

LILY. I mean, for instance. Is she as pretty as, say, other girls of her age?

TEDDY. She measures up just fine.

LILY. But she's not as pretty, say, as me?

TEDDY. She looks like my wife.

LILY. I see. Wives, of course, are never as pretty as other women.

TEDDY. Who told you that?

LILY. My mama told me that. And she should know. Does Eleanor shave her legs?

TEDDY. What kind of a question is that?

LILY. I have to shave every week. My grandmother says when girls start shaving, that's the end of *that*.

TEDDY. What's 'that?'

LILY. You're sweating, Teddy. Are you sick? Don't get sick on me because I'm in your trust. Have you ever watched your daughter take a bath?

TEDDY. Let's lay off the questions, Lily. I'm not feeling so hot.

LILY. If you had watched her bathe, you'd have known if she shaved. I'm just asking a question, Teddy.

TEDDY. Why don't you tell me what it is you'd like to do when you grow up.

LILY. I want to be an ex-Marine.

TEDDY. Don't josh me.

LILY. I like to fight. Marines get into some good scrapes, don't they?

TEDDY. Depends on what Marine's involved.

LILY. I'm going to be a composer.

TEDDY. So. Tell me about . . . musical meter.

LILY. *You* know my father best of all, Mr. T. R. Hayes. You can tell me something I don't know about him.

TEDDY. Sure I could. Tell me what you know about music.

LILY. Music is like . . . watching sex. Just watching it. Yeah. All your ex-Marine muscles bulging. And the sweat. You're sweating like a pig, Teddy. That sweat on your arms is like tiny notes jumping between the staves. *That's* what I know about music.

TEDDY. I'm too cold to sweat.

LILY. I'd like to meet Eleanor some day. Being as I am prettier than her. I'd say to her, 'Eleanor, you've got the handsomest father on earth. Such a nice looking man, that Teddy Hayes.' That's what I'd say to Eleanor.

TEDDY. Tell me some more about the sweat on my arms.

    LILY *touches* TEDDY'*s arm.*

LILY. See? This sweat droplet . . . right here. It's an 'A' natural. And this one. You know what this one is?

TEDDY. Tell me.

LILY. It's a diminished seventh. A mystery chord. Do you believe I know what I'm talking about?

TEDDY. Ain't you just a little cold out here? We could go inside. I'll buy you a hot chocolate.

LILY. Nothing open, Teddy Hayes. Do you think I'm fat?

TEDDY. You're thin as a rail, Lily Ross. Why, you're positively . . . diminished.

LILY. It was my birthday a couple of weeks ago. Maybe that's of interest to you. I'm fourteen, Teddy.

TEDDY. Eleanor is fifteen.

LILY. Wish me a happy birthday, Teddy.

TEDDY. Happy birthday, Lily.

    TEDDY *touches* LILY'*s breasts.*

LILY. It's not so cold today.

TEDDY. We can make more . . . small talk. We could.

LILY. I don't know how to make small talk.

TEDDY *removes* LILY's *blouse.*

LILY. Know who was born on my birthday, Teddy?

TEDDY. Lots of people. Tell me. I don't know.

LILY. Albert Camus. Madame Curie. Billy Graham.

TEDDY. I'm impressed.

LILY. Who was born on *your* birthday, Teddy?

TEDDY. I was, Lily. I was.

TEDDY *draws* LILY *into a kiss. He unzips his fly.* SLOAN ROSS *enters. He wears a tuxedo. He sports a neatly trimmed moustache. He watches* TEDDY *and* LILY *as lights fade from them.*

JENNY *enters. As usual, she wears her black cocktail dress.*

JENNY. Hello, Sloan. You're early tonight.

SLOAN. I've won a research award.

JENNY. That's nice.

SALLY *and* LILY *enter. Unobserved, they watch* SLOAN *and* JENNY.

JENNY. You like me in black, don't you?

SLOAN. Do I?

JENNY. Yes. Black is . . . slimming. You like that.

SLOAN. You look like a cocktail waitress. I'm going away for a few days.

JENNY *unzips her dress. It falls to the floor.*

JENNY. I'll wear pink. Lily thinks I should wear pink.

SLOAN. Put your dress on.

LILY *turns away.*

SALLY. You gotta watch this, Lily. They're getting to the good part.

LILY. No, grandma. It's not right.

SALLY slaps her, forces her to watch.

SALLY. *I* decide what's right for you. Watch your mama, Lily. Watch and learn.

JENNY. Help me, Sloan. Help me clothe myself.

SLOAN. I can't. I'm going away now.

JENNY. Where you going, honey?

SLOAN. Someplace else.

JENNY. I'm cold, baby. My dress is on the floor. Can you help me with it, Sloan?

SLOAN picks up JENNY's dress, pulls it up over her hips, her waist. JENNY takes his hands into her own hands.

JENNY. Touch me.

SLOAN. I am touching you.

JENNY (*places his hands on her breasts*). Here.

SLOAN. I'm going away.

JENNY (*places his hands between her legs*). And here.

SLOAN. Turn around.

JENNY does. SLOAN lifts up her slip. He forces her to bend over at the waist. LILY starts after them.

SALLY. Are you out of your FUCKING MIND?

LILY. I . . . I have to save her.

SALLY. She don't know she has to be saved.

Lights down on SLOAN and JENNY. LILY begins to cry. SALLY cradles her.

SALLY. When you was little, your poppy Phil and me took you to the Copacabana. And you felt just like this, all rolled up in a tiny ball, huddling against me. We packed you up in an A & P shopping bag and took you right past the bouncer. You be careful of men with moustaches, Lily. They have secrets.

SALLY *exits.*

Music in: a slow, sultry, instrumental bar tune.

MARTHA *enters. She carries a drink.*

MARTHA. You don't talk much, do you?

LILY *shrugs.*

MARTHA. Been four hours and fifteen minutes by my watch. What's it by yours?

LILY *shrugs.*

MARTHA. I like to think I can name any woman's drink on the spot. Yours would be . . . scotch. Definitely scotch. Chivas?

LILY *shakes her head, 'no.'*

MARTHA. Johnny Red? Black? Perhaps . . . Dewars? A little White Label for the lady?

LILY. Pinch.

MARTHA. Ah. Nice. Somewhat pretentious. But nice.

LILY. Actually, it's all the same to me. What's your drink?

MARTHA. Brandy Alexander. House brandy.

LILY. I've never had a Brandy Alexander. I understand it tastes like candy.

MARTHA. Want to try it?

LILY. Four hours and . . . thirteen minutes. Your watch is fast.

MARTHA. So. My watch is fast. You're very pretty. What next?

LILY. Of course, my watch might very well be slow.

MARTHA. Could be. You're nervous. And remarkably pretty. How old are you?

LILY. Then again, bar clocks are always set ten minutes fast. We both lose. I'm twenty-four. Or twenty-five.

MARTHA. Do I take my pick?

LILY. If you'd like. There's some mystery attached to the circumstances surrounding my birth. Or so they tell me.

MARTHA. Well. You don't drink Brandy Alexanders, you don't talk terribly much, and you don't know how old you are. What *do* you do?

LILY. I like to . . . watch. Sometimes.

MARTHA. And are you here to watch, or to participate?

LILY. That would depend upon whatever the participation calls for.

MARTHA. Well, I myself am a particularly adept observer.

LILY. Then I guess you're here to watch. And not to participate.

MARTHA. I can be persuaded to learn. To participate. That is, Miss –

LILY. Ramona. Ross. Miss Ramona-Ross.

MARTHA. I wish you were about . . . thirty-five. But I bet you really are twenty-five. They tell me I've a weakness for younger women.

LILY. Who are 'they?'

MARTHA. Oh . . . the same people who claim the mysterious circumstances surrounding your birth. Is Ramona your first name?

LILY. No. It's a family name. My mother's maiden name. My name is Lily Ross. Although I've preferred it to be Ramona.

MARTHA. Names are easily changed, Miss Ross. Especially here. I'm afraid I've no such thoughts about my own name. Martha McKenzie, of obviously Anglican descent.

They shake hands.

LILY. Are you also able to judge a woman by her handshake?

MARTHA. I like to try.

LILY. And how does mine measure up?

MARTHA. Admirably. And I'd guess you are . . . a singer?

LILY. Not likely, Miss McKenzie.

MARTHA. An . . . architect? Spy? Young woman with a past?

Well. I'm a photographer. For your information, that is.

LILY. I'm a . . . university professor.

MARTHA. No kidding. And what is it that you teach?

LILY. Butterfly collecting.(*A beat.*) I work in a gift shop.

MARTHA. Good. I browse in gift shops.

LILY. They tell me I've a weakness for tourists. And for older women.

They kiss. SLOAN ROSS *enters. He is, as always, tuxedoed. He carries a podium and cuts between* LILY *and* MARTHA *on his entrance.*

MARTHA exits.

LILY. Wait a minute. WAIT A MINUTE.

SLOAN *sets down his podium and faces the audience. He clears his throat.*

SLOAN. Good evening, ladies and gentlemen.

LILY. I don't want to hear your voice, daddy. Not now.

SLOAN. There is, in existence at this very moment, well over 100,000 species of Lepidoptera. This is the second largest insect order in the world, exceeded only by Coleoptera, the beetles. As this is an audience comprised largely of laymen, I shall avoid the use of technical terminology.

Quite an amazing statistic, as I am sure you will agree. It is inevitable that any large group of plant eaters as the Lepidoptera should be eaten by a great variety of other animals. Small mammals eat them directly.

Many bacteria and viruses attack the Lepidoptera and this, certainly, causes vast mortality. The Lepidoptera are not able to resist attack with the strong jaws or hard shells of other insect orders. Instead, they make cases in which they live during critical periods. Extremely important are adaptations of colour and form which enable them to escape the notice of their enemies.

CHRISTINE, THE COUNTESS VAN DYNE, *enters. She is elaborately and carefully dressed. She's the feather boa and white glove type. She speaks with a very pronounced Queens (New York) accent.*

CHRISTINE. *C' est bon*, Sloan. *Les bon mots.*

SLOAN. Well . . . I try to make my lectures as entertaining as possible.

CHRISTINE. You'll be a sensation, Sloanie.

LILY. Who is this woman?

SLOAN. There's more, Christine: The Hairstreak. There are hundreds of Hairstreaks, found chiefly in temperate and tropical regions. A remarkable feature is a bright orange and black eyespot at the anal angle of the hindwing. You might be interested to know that Hairstreaks show a marked tendency toward cannibalism.

CHRISTINE. I don't think I *comprend*, Sloan.

SLOAN. Well. They. They . . . um . . . eat. Each other. It's very simple.

LILY. I want to know who this woman is and why you've taken me here.

CHRISTINE. But Sloan, it is so . . . *degutant*. I would not bring it up in *my* lecture.

SLOAN. I've worked particularly hard on this one, Christine.

LILY (*touches* SLOAN). Daddy. Introduce me. Please.

SLOAN. Ah, Lily. I would like you to meet Christine.

LILY. Who is she?

SLOAN. Why, Lily, she's my friend.

CHRISTINE. Ahhhh . . . *ici, ma cherie.*

SLOAN. And she is also a friend of Teddy's.

LILY (*to* CHRISTINE). You know Teddy?

CHRISTINE. Yes. I have heard so very much about you, Lily.

LILY. What is your name?

SLOAN. Christine is a Countess, Lily.

CHRISTINE. (*extending a gloved hand*). I am Christine, the Countess Van Dyne. A pleasure to meet you, Lily.

LILY. I've never met a Countess.

SLOAN. Lily: don't be rude to the Countess. Kiss her hand.

CHRISTINE. *Mais oui.* It is the official greeting of Countesses.

LILY *kisses* CHRISTINE'*s hand.*

LILY. Your glove is very . . . soft. Where do you live?

CHRISTINE. *J' habite* Queens.

SLOAN. Christine has a boat and a house on the water. Wouldn't you like to see the boat, Lily?

LILY. I've never been on a boat. Do you know my mother?

CHRISTINE. Sloanie . . . ?

SLOAN. Christine is *my* friend, Lily. She doesn't know your mother. You understand.

LILY. Of course. What do you do for a living, Miss, um, Countess?

SLOAN. Christine is a dancer, Lily.

LILY. Oh. A ballerina.

CHRISTINE. Oh, nonono, *ma petite.* I dance *le Jazz.*

SLOAN. She works in a . . . club. Near her home.

LILY. A waterfront dance club?

CHRISTINE. Something like that. *Oui.*

LILY. Why do you speak French like that?

SLOAN. Lily. Don't be rude.

CHRISTINE. It's all right, Sloanie. She's got a right to ask. All Countesses are required to speak *français.*

LILY. I see. How come Teddy never talks about you?

CHRISTINE. Because, *ma petite chou,* it seems he has more urgent business with you. *Non?*

LILY. Possibly.

SLOAN. Well. We're running late, Lily, and we really must go if we're to make the lecture on time. I hope that you and the Countess will meet again. Under less . . . hurried circumstances.

LILY (*to* CHRISTINE). You're beautiful.

CHRISTINE. Why . . . *merci*. Truly.

SLOAN. Do you know how to get home from here, Lily?

LILY. Yes.

SLOAN. Very well, then. Shall we, Christine?

SLOAN *offers his arm to* CHRISTINE. *They begin to exit.* CHRISTINE *stops to drape her feather boa around* LILY's *neck.*

CHRISTINE. *A bientot, ma pauvre.*

They exit.

LILY. There's a game that children play when they mean to be especially cruel, and it goes like this: if you step on the crack, you will break your mother's back.

Sloanie, my father, taught me this game when I was five years old. We're on our way to Lenox Hill hospital. It's visit the sick mommy day. Of course, she's not . . . really sick. She's someplace between pretending and death. But how could I have known that at the time? It's early April and I am dressed in Navy blue. A Sunday. My daddy's got these . . . huge hands. Like bear paws. And he takes my miniature Lily-hands in his paws, and we begin to run. I can't keep up with him. For each step he takes, I take four or five. I'm terrified of messing my new blue suit. I can't breathe anymore and I think I surely will die. Just as I think I might fall to the sidewalk, daddy squeezes my hand even tighter and he begins to sing: if you step on the crack, you will break your mother's back.

Sing-song. Extraordinarily rhythmical. So terrified is the young Lily of tripping concrete cracks. I wish I might fly. But faster, faster we go. And when, at the end of our sadistic run, I do step on that crack, I know my breath will come no more. I have killed my mother.

This father of mine will not allow me to hold him. No contact is Lily permitted. 'Baby girl,' he says, 'my only girl, it's a game.'

MARTHA enters. She carries music paper and fudge.

MARTHA. I made you some fudge. And I bought you some music paper.

LILY. Martha, I'd like to take everything backwards. Run it in reverse. Just for a second.

MARTHA. Will you talk to me now? Please.

LILY. Yes. I'm ready.

Music in: Mozart's Twinkle, Twinkle Little Star . . . variations.

JENNY and SALLY enter. JENNY wears a wedding dress and carries a spray of delicate flowers.

SALLY. Never trust a man with a moustache, Jenny. They have secrets.

JENNY. I'd like my first child to be a boy. They're easier to care for, don't you think? But I don't really have a preference. I want a large family.

LILY. If I tell you . . . if I . . . can tell you what happened . . . you must believe me.

MARTHA. I want to believe you.

MARTHA eats some fudge.

LILY. May I have some?

MARTHA gives LILY some fudge. They eat in silence.

SALLY. He's late. The bastard's late. Brides are late, Jenny. Not grooms.

JENNY. Think of it, mother. Our children will be beautiful. When Sloan's tour of duty is up, we're going to move someplace exciting. Rome. Vienna. I'll resume my voice lessons.

MARTHA. Lily . . . talk to me.

LILY. Run, mama. Run away. He's late.

MARTHA. Lily. Lily, what's going on?

> SLOAN *and* TEDDY *enter. They are tuxedoed and beaming.* CHRISTINE *trails in behind them. She carries a bottle of champagne.*

SLOAN. Jennifer, darling. I'm sorry to be late. But it could not have been avoided.

CHRISTINE. *Bon! Bon!* I love weddings.

SALLY. We could have gone, Jenny. Now it's too fucking late.

LILY. Too late.

MARTHA. What's too late?

SLOAN. Good afternoon, Mrs. Ramona. My apologies. Allow me to present my best man, Teddy Roosevelt Hayes.

SALLY. Oh yeah? Why don't you marry this guy, Jenny. At least he's clean shaven.

LILY. Martha, do you understand that if there was a way to stop them, I would?

MARTHA. I think so. But you must understand that it's never possible.

> JACKSON *enters. He carries a bible.*

JACKSON. If there is one among you who objects to this union of kindred souls, let him speak now.

LILY. OBJECTION.

MARTHA. Lily. Baby, hold me. Let me hold you.

SALLY. It's the end of your road, Jenny.

> SLOAN *and* JENNY *join hands.*

JENNY. Our children will grow to do great things.

SLOAN. Well, I'm . . . not sure how I feel about children. Immediately, that is.

JENNY. What do you mean, Sloan?

JACKSON. In the presence of these various . . . friends . . . and relatives, I now pronounce you –

LILY. OBJECTION.

JACKSON. – man and wife. Objection overruled.

CHRISTINE applauds, throws confetti.

SALLY. You shoulda married this guy with three names when you had the chance. What difference does it make?

JENNY and SLOAN kiss.

JENNY. Do you really not want any children, Sloan?

SLOAN. We'll . . . see. We have time.

TEDDY. Awww. Sloanie's a softie, Jenny. He'll come around. I know how you feel. I love kids. Always have.

JENNY throws her flowers to LILY. They land at LILY's feet. She picks them up, gives them to MARTHA.

MARTHA. They're very pretty, Lily. Where'd you get them?

LILY. Martha. Listen to me. My mother asked me to kill her.

Blackout.

The Mozart plays on, full volume.

End of Act One.

Act Two

From the darkness, JENNY *sings.*

JENNY. 'Come sweetheart mine
  Don't sit and pine
  Tell me of the cares that make you feel so blue.
  What have I done
  Answer me hon
  Have I ever said an unkind word to you?'

  Lights up on JENNY *and* SALLY. JENNY *stands on a table and holds a knife to her lips as if it were a microphone.*

JENNY. 'My love is true
  And just for you
  I'd do almost anything at any time.
  Dear when you sigh
  Or when you cry
  Something seems to grip this very heart of mine.'

  Lights up on LILY *and* JACKSON. LILY *smokes a cigarette.*

JACKSON. Tell me what you know about the American Family, Lily.

LILY. I know nothing. I'm not part of an American family.

JENNY. Shit. I forget what comes next. What comes next, mother?

SALLY. Forget it. You ain't no singer, baby.

JACKSON. I'm asking you to theorise, Lily. For instance, you are aware of the national averages, are you not? Two and a half kids, a mortgaged home approximately twenty miles from a major city. Something like that.

LILY. Is that what you come from?

JACKSON. No. And neither do you. Nobody I know does.

JENNY. I remember the words. I do. Listen:

> 'Smile my honey dear
> While I kiss away each tear
> Or else I shall be melancholy, too.'

SALLY. It's time for your feeding.

JENNY. I'm not hungry.

SALLY. You're wasting away.

JENNY. I'm fat. I have to learn that song.

JACKSON. See, Lily, what I find interesting is that for all the talk about means and averages, most folks I know don't fit the mold.

LILY. Do you think I smoke well, counsellor?

JACKSON. Funny thing is, lots of people pretend to be in the ranks of the average. Yes, they'll tell you, I *do* have one and a half brothers. I *did* live in Massapequa Park. But when questions begin to roll, you learn that there was no Buick station wagon with wood-panelled doors. And the half brother is retarded, stashed away with his grandma in Allentown, P.A. Or else he's selling roses to motorists on the Brooklyn-Queens Expressway. Yes. You smoke exceptionally well. Most criminals do.

LILY. You think I'm a criminal.

JACKSON. Of course I do. What would you call yourself?

SALLY. Goddamn you, Jenny. You'll eat. You will.

SALLY *takes the knife away from* JENNY.

SALLY. Get down. Now.

JENNY *does.* SALLY *ties a gigantic bib around* JENNY's *neck.*

SALLY. Sit. (JENNY *does.*) Good girl.

SALLY, *ladle in hand, feeds* JENNY *out of a pot. She has to force the food down.*

JENNY (*spitting out food as she sings*). 'Come to me my melancholy baby . . . what have I DONE . . . answer me HON . . . '

SALLY *throws the pot of food onto* JENNY'*s lap.*

SALLY. I was the singer. You understand? You stole the notes right out of my mouth.

LILY. I began to smoke after I moved in with Martha. I knew it would annoy her. It was nice to be in a situation where something I did actually upset somebody else.

SALLY. I want to go to Florida.

JENNY *giggles.*

SALLY. You think that's funny?

JENNY *laughs louder.*

SALLY. I am OLD, Jenny. When people get old, their children are supposed to take care of them. I get old and I have to take care of YOU. You think that's funny?

JENNY. It's the best joke I've ever heard.

JENNY *laughs uncontrollably.*

Lights down on SALLY *and* JENNY.

JACKSON. What do you think about my theory?

LILY. About smoking? Or about families?

JACKSON. Well. If nobody I know comes from an average American family, and if nobody *they* know comes from one, and so on, who compiled the data about national averages?

LILY. Whoever had the most to gain by the data.

JACKSON. Where are all the folks with two and a half blonde and perfect children? Where do they hide?

LILY. I don't know. Maybe they all live in the same place. You tell me.

JACKSON. Do you know who James Ruppert is?

LILY. Certainly. You're talking to a true-crime expert.

JACKSON. Eleven of his relatives, including his entire

immediate family, were gathered at Mr. Ruppert's modest two-storey house in suburban Hamilton, Ohio on Easter Sunday, 1975. He led his family on an Easter egg hunt. Later, while his mother and wife were setting the table for a holiday dinner, James Ruppert loaded two .22 calibre pistols, a .357 magnum and an 18-shot rifle. Three hours later, he calmly called the police and informed them that a shooting had taken place.

LILY. Yes. He needed . . . thirty-one shots. To dispose of eleven people.

JACKSON. By all accounts, Mr. Ruppert was as average as they come.

JACKSON *exits*.

Music in: a cha-cha. CHRISTINE *enters. She dances, rather badly.*

CHRISTINE. *Un, deux*, cha-cha-cha. *Un . . . deux . . .*

LILY. When will my father be back, Countess?

CHRISTINE. Ah, my sweet, do not worry. *Attendez-vous.* Dance *le cha-cha.* A young woman needs prospects, Lily. *Le dance* is the key that unlocks many doors.

LILY. Yes. Look what it's done for you.

Music out.

CHRISTINE. *Oui.* Maybe you would like to sit outside. In the yard. You can wait for Sloan there. He won't be long.

LILY. I'm sorry. I didn't mean . . . I'm supposed to be at Mass with my father. It's Easter Sunday, you know.

CHRISTINE. Is it? I don't pay any attention to religion.

LILY. What country is your husband . . . a Count . . . in?

CHRISTINE. I've forgotten. It was a long time ago, Lily. We were young and . . . well. You know how it is.

LILY. No. I don't.

CHRISTINE. You haven't any reason to dislike me, Lily.

LILY. Oh. Where are your children?

CHRISTINE. Victor – that was the Count's name – has the children, because, to be frank, I never much cared for them. And they were boys. How was I to deal with foreign-born boys? Isn't it funny how difficult it is to get used to foreigners?

LILY. My mother wanted boys.

CHRISTINE. Victor wasn't very bright. And the children had accents. I left them all behind in Zurich.

LILY. Did you keep pictures? Baby shoes? Any reminders?

CHRISTINE. I kept the title. It's been useful.

LILY. I do like you, Christine. I do.

SLOAN and TEDDY enter. TEDDY has a bunch of flowers.

SLOAN. Lily, I've brought Teddy along to help us celebrate the holiday.

TEDDY. Hiya, Lily. You like flowers, don't you?

LILY (*to* CHRISTINE). Teach me to dance.

Lights down on CHRISTINE, SLOAN and TEDDY.

LILY. My father kept a picture of Christine in his wallet. A dancer by virtue of one badly creased photograph that frames a woman who looks very much like Christine, but younger. So young. She wears a spangled bathing suit and fishnet stockings. In her hair is a gardenia. She wears tap shoes. Behind this picture in my father's wallet was hidden a photograph of five-year-old Lily: eyes unfocused, tiny red mouth fixed in an uncomfortable grin. I took Christine's picture from Sloan's wallet. He assumed he'd lost it, like most other things in his life. For daddy, I left the photo of young Lily, hidden, at last, by nothing.

Lights up on SALLY and JENNY. SALLY is sterilising a knife with a lighter. JENNY holds out a bare arm to her mother.

SALLY. I shoulda thought of this before.

JENNY. Yeah. Hey, Lily-pie, you gonna come to Florida with us?

LILY. I want you to reconsider this, mama.

SALLY. Whatsa matter, Lily. Got a problem with sunny weather?

LILY. My mother's place is here.

JENNY. I lost my place.

SALLY. We're gonna have a fine time in the sunshine. Give me your hand, Jenny.

LILY. What are you doing?

SALLY. Ain't you never heard of blood sisters?

LILY. You're not sisters.

JENNY. It doesn't matter.

SALLY *cuts* JENNY's *thumb, then her own. They press their thumbs together.*

SALLY. Swear it now, Jenny.

JENNY. I swear.

SALLY. Say: I swear to God I'll go to Florida with my mother.

JENNY. I swear to God I'll go to Florida with my mother.

SALLY. I swear to leave my husband and daughter behind.

JENNY. I . . . swear. To leave.

LILY. How will you get there? Where will you live? You haven't any money.

SALLY. She'll find a job. And she'll take care of me.

LILY. She's incapable of working.

JENNY. I used to be a switchboard operator.

LILY. She'll explode on impact. She'll get off the Greyhound and explode, like a grenade.

SALLY. Listen, Lily. She made me a promise.

JENNY. I made her a promise.

LILY. I don't want you to leave.

JENNY. You're old enough. Go out, Lily. Leave me. It's

supposed to happen. How old are you now? Twenty . . . thirty.

LILY. Twenty-five.

SALLY. Twenty-five, she works in a store that sells tee-shirts. Hot stuff. Star material.

JENNY. Yeah. A big zero.

SALLY. A leech. She sucks us dry, Jenny. Come on. Swear to me. Do it.

JENNY. A major disappointment. How old did you say you were, Lily? Forty-six? Twelve? Seventy-seven?

SALLY. A big nothing. I'm really gonna enjoy being taken care of.

LILY. I'm twenty-five. And I'm moving out.

JENNY. She's moving out.

SALLY. You hear that? She's walking out on you, Jenny. The nerve. You raise a kid, they eat your food, they walk out on you. I wouldn't allow it.

LILY. You *didn't* allow it, grandma.

JENNY. I . . . I . . . get my chart, Lily. My pressure. Where's my chart?

LILY. Yeah. I'm moving out. I met someone. A woman.

SALLY. You what? You met a *what?*

LILY. A woman. She reminds me of daddy's girlfriend, Christine. You know Christine, mama, don't you?

JENNY. I swear, I swear, I swear, I swear . . .

SALLY. You met a fucking *woman?*

LILY. I have a picture of Christine, mama. She's awfully pretty. Would you like to see?

JENNY. I swear. I do swear. I'll go to Florida and leave my husband and daughter behind.

MARTHA *enters.*

MARTHA. Have you ever made love to a woman, Lily?

LILY. Here, mama. A bon voyage gift. From me to you.

LILY gives JENNY the picture of CHRISTINE.

MARTHA. You seemed so . . . experienced. In the bar. Don't get me wrong. I don't mind.

JENNY (*looking at the photograph*). Is she . . . some kind of athlete?

LILY. She's a dancer.

SALLY. I've never seen anything like this. Your daughter's telling you she's a DYKE.

JENNY. Really? Well, she's entitled. She's . . . what? Fifty-five? She's old enough.

LILY. Good-bye, mama.

LILY goes to MARTHA.

MARTHA. I thought you were the teacher.

LILY. No. I like to watch. Remember?

JENNY shows SALLY the picture of CHRISTINE.

JENNY. Nice looking, isn't she?

SALLY. When are we leaving? I gotta pack, you know.

JENNY. Soon. We'll leave soon.

SALLY. When?

JENNY. Later, mother. Later.

Lights down on JENNY and SALLY.

MARTHA. It's easy.

LILY. Show me.

MARTHA. Take off your blouse.

LILY does. MARTHA reaches out for her, and LILY turns, her back to MARTHA.

MARTHA. Interesting. Do you always make love with your back to your partner?

LILY. Yes. Is there something wrong with that?

MARTHA. Well . . . it's kind of odd.

LILY. WHAT'S WRONG WITH IT.

MARTHA touches LILY. LILY pulls away.

MARTHA. Hey . . . it's okay. I'm not going to hurt you.

LILY puts on her blouse.

LILY. I guess you want me to leave.

MARTHA. No. I don't. Stay a while.

LILY. Why? What do you want?

MARTHA. Nothing. You. Whatever.

LILY. Do you dance?

MARTHA. No. I . . . well, I never really have.

LILY. Good.

MARTHA. Is this a test?

LILY. Yes.

MARTHA. And did I supply the correct answer?

LILY. Yes. You did. Do you like . . . sunshine?

MARTHA. Sure. I guess I do. Don't you?

LILY. No. I like winter. I like to shiver. Builds character.

MARTHA. Lily, listen. I don't know . . . what to do now. I'm
very attracted to you. I'd like to . . . touch you. Hold you.
Something.

LILY. Wouldn't you like to know what I know about music? I
know a lot about music, Martha.

MARTHA kisses LILY.

MARTHA. Let me take you to bed.

LILY. I had a lover once.

MARTHA. What happened?

LILY. The choice was me, or his friendship with my father. He
chose my father. Everyone does.

MARTHA. I haven't. I don't even know your father.

LILY. Don't you find it strange? I've just told you something quite out of the ordinary.

MARTHA. Not really. There's always a story more bizarre than your own.

JENNY enters. She carries a can of shaving cream and a razor.

LILY. I'd like to show you how to dance.

MARTHA. All right.

Lights up on SLOAN. He's sleeping, slumped back in a chair. His tux is a mess.

LILY and MARTHA waltz. They are initially unsure of each other, unsure of each other's body.

JENNY approaches the sleeping form of SLOAN. She caresses his face, touches his lips. She kisses his forehead.

LILY and MARTHA's dance becomes more graceful, more steady. They are enjoying themselves.

JENNY. Truth is, Sloan, I don't know *what* you do. Never have. My mother calls you the Bug Man. And maybe she's right. You are so very handsome. Lily left today. Yes, she's gone. Where? Oh, well, I don't know. I didn't think it appropriate to ask. Do you really mean it, Sloan? We'll go away? I know, darling. I know you don't love that woman. Yes, I do look marvellous in black. You're absolutely right.

JENNY applies shaving cream to SLOAN's moustache. She shaves it off.

MARTHA and LILY's dance becomes a passionate embrace. MARTHA's hands are all over LILY's body, exploring it, becoming accustomed to it.

JENNY. It had to come off, Sloan. My mother says it contained secrets.

Blackout.

Slide display:

LILY and SLOAN, holding hands on the beach.

JENNY, *posing with her knife as a microphone.*

A black-and-white police photo of the Ross kitchen, blood everywhere.

The photo of CHRISTINE *in bathing suit and fishnet stockings.*

Lights up on JACKSON.

JACKSON. Shortly thereafter, ladies and gentlemen, Sloan Ross left his wife and set up house with the Countess. Sally Ramona did not make it to Florida. Life at the walk-up remained untouched by the world at large.

LILY *enters, wheeling a hospital table upon which lies* SALLY RAMONA. SALLY *is hooked up to an i.v.*

JACKSON. Ladies and gentlemen, allow me to present the defendant's grandmother.

SALLY (*with great difficulty*). Butter . . . flies.

JACKSON. Mrs. Ramona refers to the second largest insect order in the world.

SALLY. Never. Trust a man. With a moustache.

JACKSON. Mrs. Ramona refers to the defendant's father, Sloan Ross.

SALLY. STIG . . . MA . . . TA . . .

JACKSON. Mrs. Ramona refers to the Ross' traditionally Catholic upbringing of their daughter, Lily.

SALLY *very suddenly sits bolt upright and begins pulling the i.v.tubes away from her body. She addresses* LILY *directly.*

SALLY. MANSLAUGHTER . . . MANSLAUGHTER . . . MANSLAUGHTER.

LILY. It's the pig woman. Come to claim me for her own.

SALLY. I ain't no pig woman. I came to clean your mother's blood.

LILY. Jane Gibson. Also known as the pig woman.

SALLY. I AIN'T NO PIG WOMAN.

SALLY *crawls around the floor. She scrubs the floor with her palms.*

SALLY. I had to scrub Jenny's blood from the floor. Look. See that? I'm scrubbing this spot, see? And it up and disappears on me. The blood is jumping around the linoleum and I can't catch it and I think I'm going crazy but no. No. It's really happening. A blood vessel in my head pops. I hear it. Like it's mocking me. I'm having a fucking stroke. TAKE CARE OF ME.

Lights down on SALLY.

LILY *tries to touch the projected image of* CHRISTINE, *but it disappears.*

MARTHA *enters.*

MARTHA. Lily, what did you mean? What did you mean when you told me your mother asked you to kill her?

SLOAN, *now clean shaven, and* CHRISTINE *enter.*

SLOAN. Lily, why did you wait so long to leave home?

TEDDY *enters.*

TEDDY. Hey, Lily, what's the deal with your old dyke friend?

MARTHA. I am not old.

LILY. Jackson. What if?

JACKSON. What if . . . what?

LILY. What if. This never happened.

JACKSON. Ah. Yes. Everybody wants to play that game, Lily. Trouble is, nobody knows how to make it work. Go ahead. Try. You're on your own, Lily.

JACKSON *exits.*

Lights down on all but LILY.

LILY. My father is a renowned lepidopterist. My mother attends each of his lectures and she understands everything he says. Of course, she's very busy herself, being as she's rather a good mezzo-soprano. Just a cut below super stardom, but she does well. She's in demand.

My grandmother, once a famous mezzo herself, has retired to Fort Lauderdale. And because she's very wealthy, men pursue her. She's dazzling.

Lights up on SALLY. *She reclines in a beach chair. She wears a bathing suit.*

SALLY. Hiya, Lily. Why don't you come down here with your husband and sons? I've got a big brick house with a portable patio. And guess what? I've got the best fucking tan in the world.

Lights down on SALLY.

LILY. My dearest friend is the world-famous flamenco dancer, Christine. She and her husband, the Danish count Victor Van Dyne, frequently host dinner parties for my parents. When they're in town, that is.

Lights up on CHRISTINE, *in flamenco costume.*

CHRISTINE. *Merci. Merci, mes amis.* And now, for my fifteenth encore, I shall dance a bolero.

Lights down on CHRISTINE.

LILY. I, of course, marry John-John Kennedy and I bear him five sons. He is busy with law school and fund-raisers, which leaves me time to be with Martha McKenzie, my one true love. Martha and I often travel.

Lights up on MARTHA. *She's surrounded by luggage and cameras.*

MARTHA. Lily, I've got our itinerary. We land in Rome, where we'll spend four days at the Hotel Flora. We train from Rome to Venice, where we spend three weeks at the Danieli. After that, of course, you've got to be in London for the premiere of your new opera.

Lights down on MARTHA.

LILY. Oh, yes. And in between my various engagements, I find the time to complete my sixth opera. It's the one I'm writing for my mother. She's really looking forward to it. Lastly, I have set up a trust fund for Eleanor Roosevelt Hayes, daughter of my father's friend and my godfather, Teddy

Roosevelt Hayes. Eleanor wants to be a composer, too. Teddy's proud of the example I've set for her. He's such a nice man.

Lights up on TEDDY. *He wears sweat clothes and lifts weights.*

TEDDY. Thanks for the gym, Lily. A guy's got to stay in shape as he gets older. My wife really appreciates it, too.

Lights down on TEDDY.

LILY. Who says you can't have everything?

Lights up on JENNY. *She looks older, greyer. Her hair's a mess. She wears an old hospital robe and fluffy slippers. She tries to brush her hair, but can't quite do it.*

Lights up on SLOAN. *He carries a gun.*

SLOAN. Hello, Lily. How've you been?

LILY. I manage. We manage.

SLOAN. How's the gift shop?

LILY. How's Christine?

SLOAN. Fine. She's fine. She asks about you.

LILY. Give her my best, daddy. I'm going to see mama today.

SLOAN. Do you need money, Lily? Are you supporting yourself?

LILY. Martha does okay.

SLOAN. I see. Well. How's the, uh, music?

LILY. Can't complain. I have lots of blank music paper.

SLOAN. Give it time. It'll come.

LILY. No. It won't. I don't really know how to read music, much less write it. I just know . . . tidbits. Interesting facts. Trivia.

SLOAN. I'd like to help you, Lily. But I'm a little short of cash. Christine, well, she has expensive habits.

LILY. Does it bother you, daddy?

SLOAN. What?

LILY. Me. And Martha. Mama. Teddy. Pick one.

SLOAN. What's to be bothered by?

LILY. I just wondered. What's that?

SLOAN. A luger. It's very old and valuable. It's . . . I want to give it to you. It's worth quite a bit.

LILY *takes the gun.*

LILY. A foreign gun.

SLOAN. Yes?

LILY. Christine mustn't like it. It being a foreigner. You know.

SLOAN *laughs.*

SLOAN. Yes. Well. I must go now. I have a class.

LILY. Thanks, daddy.

SLOAN. Oh, it's nothing. Really.

LILY. I'm thanking you generally. I want to know what it feels like to thank your parent for something.

SLOAN *exits.*

LILY (*to the audience*). My father kept a luger by his bedside. In case he ever felt like shooting a butterfly.

JENNY. Lily-pie, will you fix your mama's hair?

LILY. Yes, mama. I will. I always have.

JENNY. It was your forty-fifth birthday yesterday, wasn't it? I'm sorry I didn't send a card.

LILY. No, mama. My birthday is in November. It was your birthday yesterday.

JENNY. It was? That's funny. Your grandmother didn't mention it. How's your husband? What was his name? Martin?

LILY. He's fine, mama.

JENNY. Are you pregnant yet?

LILY. No mama, not yet.

JENNY. When?

LILY. Soon.

JENNY. I entered a contest, Lily. I saw it in the newspaper and had your grandma cut it out. I enter a lot of contests. Sweepstakes. Look-alike competitions.

LILY. That's nice, mama. Good luck.

JENNY. Oh, I won't win, baby. I just like to enter for the recreation. I like to anticipate winning. Have you finished writing that song for me?

LILY. Oh, yes. I've written fifty songs for you, mama.

JENNY. I'm real proud of you, Lily. When will I get to sing them? I'm a little out of practice, mind you.

LILY. Soon, mama. Soon. There's time.

JENNY. Are you pregnant yet, honey?

LILY. Yes, mama. I am.

JENNY. That's lovely, Lily. I hope it's a boy. They're easier to care for.

LILY. I have two boys already, mama. Don't you remember? I'm hoping for a girl.

JENNY. That's right . . . how stupid of me. You have two boys. I knit sweaters for them.

LILY. That's right, mama. And we go for drives to the country in our Buick station wagon.

JENNY. You know, I've always liked your husband's car, Lily.

LILY. He likes it, too. We all like it.

LILY *puts the gun on a table between her and her mother*.

JENNY. What's that?

LILY. It's a gun, mama.

JENNY. Are you afraid of something, Lily?

LILY. No, mama. There's nothing to fear.

JENNY. Would you name your baby girl after me?

LILY. Of course I will.

JENNY. Listen to me. Are you listening to me, Lily?

LILY. I'm listening.

JENNY. Your daddy was a wrong number, Lily, who ought never have been answered.

LILY. I know. Why don't we take care of it so that you don't have to answer?

JENNY. Will you brush your mama's hair, sweet-pea? I like to look nice for you.

LILY. All right, mama. It's time.

LILY *takes the brush from* JENNY *and begins to brush her mother's hair.*

JENNY. What's that on the table, Lily-pie?

LILY. I told you. It's a brush.

JENNY. Oh. Would you sing one of the songs you wrote for me?

LILY. Of course. (*She begins to sing:*)
'The night was mighty dark
So you could hardly see
For the moon refused to shine.'

JENNY. I know this song, Lily. I know it.

LILY. That's because I wrote it just for you, mama. Help me sing it.

JENNY (*she sings*).

'Couple sitting underneath
A willow tree
For love they pine.'

LILY. Go on, mama. You're doing fine.

LILY *puts the brush on the table and picks up the gun. She brushes her mother's hair with the gun.*

JENNY. 'Little maid was kinda 'fraid of dark
So she said, I guess I'll go . . . '

LILY. 'The boy began to sigh
Looked up at the sky
Told the moon his little tale of woe.'

JENNY. 'Shine on, shine on harvest moon
Up in the sky
I ain't had no lovin' since
January . . . February . . . '

LILY. 'June or July.'

JENNY. There are more words, Lily. Aren't there more words?

LILY. There's always something left to be said, mama. But it's
fine. It's pretty this way.

JENNY. When will you let me meet your husband?

LILY. He'll come to your concert.

JENNY. My concert? When is it?

LILY. Next week. You're singing my songs.

JENNY. That's soon, Lily. I have to look nice. Do you think I
should wear black? It's slimming.

LILY. Whatever you'd like, mama. It's yours.

JENNY. Will it be dark?

LILY. Would you like it to be dark?

JENNY. Oh sure, honey. Everything looks better in the dark.
That's when people are their prettiest.

LILY. It's dark now, mama.

JENNY. Lily, are you here with me?

LILY. I'm here, mama.

JENNY. Don't let me go.

LILY. I'm staying.

JENNY. Don't you let me go, Lily.

LILY. I'll never let you go.

JENNY. I'm ready, baby. Hold me. It's dark. Are you singing
with me, Lily? Are you ready?

LILY. I'm ready, mama. And I'm singing at the top of my lungs. Hold tight, mama.

LILY presses the gun against her mother's head.

JENNY. I was always so interested in a family with a past. With some history.

LILY. There's nothing ahead of you but the future, mama. The future.

Blackout, as LILY *pulls the trigger.*

End of play.